❀

Welcome to your Walking Stick Press guided journal. Within these pages you'll find:

❀

instruction to guide you on your way

❀

writing prompts to lead you to your goal

❀

blank pages to record your responses to the prompts—to map your insights as you heal, grow and explore

❀

quotes to inspire, provoke and refresh you

❀

Along the way, feel free to jot in the margins, add your own quotes, let writing take you down a trail you didn't expect. Enjoy the journey.

❀

What Really Matters to Me

a guided journal

Robyn Conley-Weaver

Walking Stick Press

Cincinnati, Ohio

Visit our Web site at www.writersdigest.com for information on more
resources for writers.

ISBN 0-89879-985-6

Edited by Jack Heffron and Meg Leder
Cover and interior design by Matthew S. Gaynor
Production coordinated by Mark Griffin

✾

Dedication

In honor of each individual spirit.

✾

Acknowledgments

With sincere appreciation...

to Kathryn J. Foster, Ph.D., for her professional presence, her genuine concern for others and her psychological expertise. As a consultant, she has served as a cornerstone for this project. As a friend, she has offered unending sustenance.

to Jack Heffron, Senior Editor at Walking Stick Press, whose insightful awareness first conceived, then guided this work with skill, craft and integrity.

and to Kimberley Cameron, my amazing agent and friend, whose finesse and tender encouragement brought this project to acceptance.

✾

Table of Contents

Introduction

> Be yourself and think for yourself; and
> while your conclusions may not be
> infallible, they will be nearer right than
> the conclusions forced on you by
> those who have a personal interest in
> keeping you in ignorance.
>
> *Elbert Hubbard*
> author

Surrounded by pine trees, I could always be myself. Even their shadows in the Montana forests never bothered me until one gray afternoon when I was seven. Before that day I had savored the shadows almost as much as the sunshine. They had always welcomed my shyness, my quiet explorations, my habit of collecting prickly pinecones. But that day the lodgepole silhouettes felt cooler, filtering out much of the sun's light. My bottom lip quivered as I stood holding my pet rabbit in a box.

"But Daddy, I don't want to let Jack go."

"That's too bad, young lady. What matters to you isn't important."

I'm not important?

Shame mingled with dust from the mountain trail. I placed the cardboard box near the edge of the path and opened the lid. Jack's nose peeked out. His whiskers twitched. His tall ears stretched forward, and he bolted for the woody brush, completely at home in the rugged wilderness.

I felt the tears pool, couldn't stop them from falling. They traversed my cheeks, etching patterns for creases I see today whenever I pass a mirror. Each time I do, I'm startled back to those silent silhouettes of pines and the first day I realized that what mattered to me wasn't important.

"Stop that damn bawling, or I'll give you a real reason to cry."

I'm not supposed to cry when I'm sad?

As an adult, it's easy to understand why Jack the jackrabbit had to go. It's easy to empathize with my parents about the messes he scattered throughout our house. It's easy to believe the little critter survived quite well without me petting him and shredding cabbage for his daily meals. And yet, as an adult, some things are still difficult to comprehend.

Why, while I stood sobbing in the shadows, did nobody offer the commonsense assurances that seem so obvious now? It would have taken little extra time and little extra effort to make such logical explanations. It would have taken a little creativity perhaps to distract the child I was from the childish hurt and to offer a morsel of compassion...but why bother? After all, what really mattered to *me* wasn't important.

As a parent of two children, I can't imagine not caring about what is important to them or not doing what I can to ease their pain during the everyday stresses of life. But when I was a child, my father lived constantly on the move, seeing in tunnel vision, chasing his own life's desires. And as much as I loved my mother, she struggled daily to safeguard her sanity from the codependency and bipolar disorder she endured for years. She simply wasn't emotionally in tune with her kids.

So the phrases haunted.

I don't matter.... My feelings are wrong.... Don't cry....

The numbness in my soul spread as we lived a nomadic life, playing U-Haul tag, rarely staying in one town for more than a few months. There simply were no opportunities to foster the close friendships that may have instilled the hope that I might matter to someone.

Still, I had a secret strategy to make myself feel better. On my most prized possession—a red-covered Big Chief tablet— I wrote down the feelings nobody believed were important. In broken first-grade penmanship I scribbled words about missing Jack the jackrabbit, and I drew pictures of his new forest home.

> Writing gave life to the thoughts I wasn't allowed to speak. Writing made me feel better. Writing kept me from becoming completely numb.

Writing gave life to the thoughts I wasn't allowed to speak. Writing made me feel better. Writing kept me from becoming completely numb.

As the days wore on, and we continued to make move after move, I filled lots of pages in lots of notebooks about all the things that did matter to me—like how I felt something awesome, something powerful, when I hiked and romped in the Montana forests.

The wilderness always offered a spiritual peace that I knew no name for as a child, but one that was tangible just the same. The fallen pine needles, the aroma of dewy bark and sap, the lullaby of a mountain stream—they all wrapped me in a natural security blanket.

I hoped, by writing about the forest and the things that mattered to me, that I could hold on to a little of my own spirit. Over time, writing made me a believer in myself, even when I had to choose silence and numbness.

What I found truly interesting, even at a young age, was realizing I wrote honestly in my crude diaries. Somehow it was impossible to write anything other than truth on those blue-lined pages. Rereading them enabled me to see more sides to our whole family and gave me an honest point of view about many situations that had confused me in the past.

Writing helped me imagine what other people might be thinking—why they acted or didn't act a certain way. Years later the writing led to understanding. That more mature understanding gave way to forgiveness and eventually even compassion for both parents. After all, they most likely did the best they could based on their own upbringings.

> What I found truly interesting, even at a young age, was realizing I wrote honestly in my crude diaries. Somehow it was impossible to write anything other than truth on those blue-lined pages.

Writing also helped me lead a simpler life. Through writing down my insights, I could see where I honestly wanted to aim my energies. It helped me settle down and heal so I could evaluate on paper the chaos of my life.

I found I often made decisions for the wrong reasons. My choices were sometimes grounded in fear, sometimes grounded in routine, sometimes grounded in pleasing others rather than myself. By jotting down stresses and strategies, I was able to choose more positive uses of my time—not only to simplify my life, but also to amplify my blessings.

I learned that choosing what really matters leads to a simpler life. Choice is what grants a person profound joy.

The five sections in this book are stepping-stones that will lead you to a greater awareness of your inner self. Each section contains sample prompts to coax you into writing off the top of your head. Forget proper grammar, forget punctuation, forget sentence structure. Just toss your feelings onto the paper and see where they lead you.

If you feel yourself wandering onto a different topic, hooray! That's a terrific bonus through which you might discover some unexpected and revealing insights. Along the journey you'll feel occasional emotional ripples as you write. These are completely natural aftershocks. Sometimes the strength of these tremors can be unsettling, but they mean you're growing closer to your center—your core, to what really matters.

Writing in this journal can lead you to a simpler, more joyful life. The cost is minimal, the rewards are priceless, and the process will help you emerge from the shadows of your emotions—emotions that really do matter and will free you to be yourself.

❀

chapter 1

Acknowledging the Chaos

None of us can help the things life has
done to us. They're done before you
realize it, and once they're done they
make you do other things until at last
everything comes between you and
what you'd like to be, and you have lost
your true self forever.

Eugene O'Neill
playwright

So, what really matters to you?

Before you answer, remember that whatever is in your
heart—in the core of your soul—is what is important. No, it is
paramount. What really matters is your inner self.

Obviously your inner self is a culmination of your personal and professional priorities—a melody of your secret spirit connection and real-life responsibilities. In "Truth of
Intercourse," Robert Louis Stevenson wrote, "A little amateur
painting in water-colours shows the innocent and the quiet
mind." Your inner self is your watercolor painting of your innocent and quiet mind.

Before any authentic brush strokes can manifest from your inner self, you first have to be honest about your priorities. Writing can reveal what matters to you so you can move forward with simplifying your life.

Are you willing to work to find out why you're struggling with as many conflicting emotions as your day-planner is bulging with conflicting schedules? Excavating further, do you want to chip away at issues that will help you rid yourself of emotional decay? You may answer yes quickly, and that's fine because these are the problems that can weigh down even the simplest routine. The process takes a commitment of time and emotional energy, though, and this journal will help.

When you're ready to discover what really matters to you and how that discovery will help you lead a simpler life, then give yourself completely to these writing exercises. The act of writing combines thoughts, emotions, senses and structure—interpret this as organization—to relay a story. The exercises and journaling suggestions that follow will allow you to rehash your own personal story. They will guide you through the process of taking a few steps backward so you can go forward with confidence.

Once you realize your heartfelt priorities, you'll unlock your inner self, or Holy Spirit, or inner child. My nine-year-old daughter refers to it as her "God-self."

Kathryn J. Foster, Ph.D., is a psychologist who encourages her clients to keep a daily journal of their thoughts, feel-

> Writing can reveal what matters to you so you can move forward with simplifying your life.

ings and behaviors. She believes that writing is an excellent way to become aware of how you talk with your inner self.

> Journaling one's feelings and thoughts leads to self-discovery, helping you find out, for instance, what you say to yourself when you fail. Some will say, "That's OK; I did the best I could," or "You stupid idiot—you never do things right!" The difference will show up in your level of confidence, and it begins with your self-talk. Likewise, if all your thoughts end in "I wonder what my mother would say," then it's time to gain emotional autonomy. Often people aren't even aware of their inside worlds until they give themselves permission to write whatever it is that they feel and think.

I think it's interesting that health professionals are finally confirming what we writers have known since the beginning of the first alphabet: writing is communication with your inner self. Once you've learned to positively communicate with your inner self, you can manage stress and tap into keen insights that writing brings you.

For example, Louise DeSalvo's book *Writing As a Way Of Healing* emphasizes how writing about stressful things can help us overcome them. Her scholarly studies reveal how some famous authors have used writing as therapy to work out such issues as abuse and alcoholism. She also warns that honest soul-writing can unearth buried issues that at times may require professional therapy to help a person heal completely.

Most people aren't facing such issues. In fact, most people simply need reminders of what really mattered to them *before* they allowed society's standards for everyday life to steal their dreams. Writing can help you reconnect with your inner self—the spirit that really does matter. That reconnection is what will help you lead a simpler life.

In the introduction to her autobiography, *Me*, Katherine Hepburn wrote, "I'm my *main* gift from my parents. And when I realized this, I also knew why I had become interested in writing this book. I wanted to discover the real reason back of all the fluff. That bit of fiber which can be developed in all of us."

Each of us does have a worthy inner self back of all the fluff. It is the spirit we're born with, yet oftentimes we end up suffocating it because we listen to other people's ideas of what we should think, feel or choose. What we *should* choose is what our inner selves tell us to choose. Those choices are the natural instincts we've sometimes ignored because we've been told they're selfish.

Discovering what matters to you isn't selfish behavior; it's necessary. Any other option will make you spiritually ill and eventually contaminate every endeavor and relationship. In order to choose healthy priorities, those priorities have to matter to you.

I can't emphasize it enough: choosing what really matters to you *is* the key to leading a simpler life.

Perhaps you're at a point now where you're suffering in health and spirit because you've chosen a career that was expected of you, or chosen relationships out of fear—because you worried about what might happen if you didn't choose them.

Writing will show you that you're responsible for this mess. The truth is, to succeed you have to start with a thorough scrubbing. You must begin by taking an honest evaluation of your current emotional health. You have to be willing to accept responsibility for the place you are now and not blame that condition on anyone else.

> Journaling will help you accept your current situation and move forward to where you want to be in the future.

Journaling will help you accept your current situation and move forward to where you want to be in the future. First, glance through these prompts and choose one that appeals to you. Write down a few thoughts, even if you just end up with a hodgepodge list that might not seem to make sense at first. That's your warm-up. If you stumble after a few phrases, try other prompts until you feel more comfortable. Remember, there are no right or wrong feelings, no right or wrong ways to journal, and nobody except you to determine what really matters to you.

❀

Prompts

Choose the prompts that interest you most, and use the blank pages that follow to record your responses.

one

List five words *you* believe describe your personality (even if these traits/characteristics are not what you think others believe about you). What are the positive aspects of those descriptions? What are the negative aspects of those descriptions?

two

List five words *other* people would use to describe your personality. What are the positive aspects of those descriptions? What are the negative aspects of those descriptions?

three

Have you ever wanted to change anything about the way you are physically? Emotionally? Intellectually?

four

Make a list of the daily chores and errands that keep you out of touch with your inner self.

five

What items in your schedule keep you from focusing on what matters most to you?

six

Start two sentences with this phrase: "I am proud of myself because..."

seven

Start two sentences with this phrase: "Others are proud of me because..."

eight

Describe in a few sentences your idea of a stress-free life.

nine

Start two sentences with "I wish I could stop doing..."

ten

Write down other people's problems that cause you such anxiety that you believe you can't choose a simpler life.

eleven

What causes you the most stress on a daily basis?

twelve

What would you like to do/try/accomplish that you believe you don't have time to do?

thirteen

Write down any goals you remember having when you were a child. If any of those goals are still important to you now, explain why.

fourteen

If you woke up tomorrow without the stresses of today, what would you do with your day? List the reasons why you believe you can't make that day today.

fifteen

Pick two main stresses and two main goals you've discovered so far and assign a dollar value to them.

sixteen

If you had to pay to retain your two main stresses, would you be willing to fork over that cash each morning?

seventeen

Look at your two main goals. How can you earn the "money" necessary to buy those for your life?

14 | When we listen to our Inner
Voice, the heart speaks. Then,
and only then, can we realize
our ultimate truth.

Gwen Choate

author

Whether you think you can or
whether you think you can't—
you are right.

Henry Ford
inventor and businessman

They shall mount up with
wings like eagles; they shall
run and not be weary; they
shall walk and not faint.

Isaiah 40:31

The worst loneliness is not to
be comfortable with yourself.

Mark Twain
author and humorist

Writing is a spiritual exercise, as pleasurable as bench pressing.

Rick DeMarinis
author

God chose to put Himself
into words for us so we could
see how to put ourselves into
words for Him.

N. R. Masters
inspirational author and speaker

26 | Writing helps us identify
our spiritual energy so we
can become empowered to
succeed in this universe.

Denise Vitola
author

The harder you look at your past —with eyes to see what really happened—the greater your joy in today.

Barbara Breedlove Rollins
judge and author

Checkpoint   Your mind and emotions will crash and storm like thunderheads while you journal; it's quite common to feel exhausted after a strong writing session. Try not to allow that initial fatigue to deter you. When you've had time to rest, tackle the next section.

Remember, this book is for you to use on your own schedule and at your own rate of progression. It will submerge you as deeply into your inner self as you're willing to go. It will also tug you back to the surface and set you toward a leaner, yet truer perspective than you've ever allowed yourself to view.

Few people have taken time to plan their lives with a honed-down, simple—yet spiritual—formula. Here's your second chance to design your destiny. As Lily Tomlin once said, "I always wanted to be somebody when I grew up; I should have been more specific." This process is your opportunity to be more specific about who you want to be as you add a touch of watercolor to your self-portrait.

※

chapter 2

Accepting Responsibility

> If we let obligation, addiction,
> worry, guilt, fear, depression or
> anxiety rule us to the point that we
> concede all choice, then we have
> allowed ourselves to become slaves
> to that force. But are we ever
> truly without choice?
>
> *Kathy Jacobson*
> author

"I never really knew that about myself."

"I had no idea this bothered me so much."

Those phrases are the two most common responses I hear from people who have begun journaling toward a simpler life. They are always amazed at the core issues that pop right up when they spend a few moments writing down the nagging thoughts or stresses that have been pinballing around in their subconscious minds.

Saying those comments out loud is the first step to acknowledging responsibility for what has happened so far in their lives. It is also a necessary step toward accepting responsibility for what will come next.

One woman in a class I taught entered the room the first night complaining about her job. Her brow was creased with worry lines and at one point she shook her head, saying, "I'm so afraid I may have to quit if things don't get better at work."

At first I assumed it was the woman's workload that stressed her out, but the more she talked, I realized it wasn't her job causing the problem. It was a co-worker who constantly used this woman as a sounding board. As we went over various writing exercises and prompts in class, she began writing about specific stresses. After one particularly beneficial session, she identified the friction on her own.

She already knew that stress involving her job occupied her subconscious thoughts. What she couldn't pinpoint, however, was the amount of time she gave away to the co-worker. Not until she had written down the specifics regarding her work-related stress did she realize how often during the day she permitted the co-worker to invade her personal space. Because she worried about the productivity that each time-eating "chat" stole from her workday, the woman carried home additional tension as she left the employee parking lot each afternoon. She never rested.

This realization revitalized my student. Suddenly she saw hope and wanted to discover ways to curb the intrusions from her co-worker. We discussed strategies that she would feel comfortable trying. By the end of that night, her tension lines had eased and the first smile she'd given to the class crept from her cheeks all the way into her eyes. It was a sincere smile that started from a healthier inner self.

This woman decided to listen to the co-worker only at specific times during the workday. As those allowed conversations wound down, my student would say, "I care about you, but I'm going to put this topic into prayer now because I need to get back to work." By making this statement, she would prevent herself from feeling guilty about cutting the co-worker off, which was a concern she said she'd have if she decided to completely ignore the woman. She also believed she would be doing something positive by praying. And most importantly, she felt her decision to simplify her day and take control over her schedule was validated through the class writing exercises she had done.

As a facilitator for these types of classes, I can tell you my greatest joy comes from the follow-up discussions after these choices are made. When she returned the next week, she said, "I wish I had learned this years ago!" Her co-worker had not only respected the woman's choice, but had expressed appreciation that the woman was sincerely praying for her problems. Peace came to her office because she asked for her own time back—a decision the woman at first thought might be selfish or one she would feel guilty about.

Before you can use the insights you've gained from the first set of prompts, you have to practice saying, "I am responsible for the past use of my time and energy and the future use

> Peace came to her office because she asked for her own time back—a decision the woman at first thought might be selfish or one she would feel guilty about.

of my time and energy." My student had to realize she was allowing this woman to manipulate her workday and her thinking patterns. After she accepted responsibility for her part in the negative situation, she was able to learn ways to keep those situations from recurring. She was able to simplify her life and reclaim more time for herself.

To reclaim more of yourself, remember it's OK to continue writing more than you're prompted if you're digging into a topic. Just keep going in any direction you choose. If you happen to get stuck, you might try starting up again by writing, "When I think about this I feel...". This strategy should give you a jump start that will lead you toward a simpler life.

❀

one

Write this phrase at the top of your next journal entry: "I am responsible for the past use of my time and energy." Give specific examples of how you have used your time and energy poorly, and how you have used them well.

two

Write this phrase: "I am responsible for the future use of my time and energy." Give specific examples of what matters to you.

three

To move forward you have to please yourself. Write this phrase: "I don't have to please anyone else." Expound on situations where you have pleased others instead of yourself.

four

Give specific examples of tangible goals you would want to achieve if you could do what matters to you.

five

Write this phrase: "I have the power to choose what really matters and to go forward." Give an example of how you can use that power.

six

List the things in your life that don't really matter to you and that sap your time and energy. (Some will be obvious, such as work and home responsibilities.)

seven

List the invisible energy-drainers, such as worries concerning problems you have no ability to solve.

eight

List all the nonsense things that steal your time—even watching television.

Prompts

Choose the prompts that interest you most, and use the blank pages that follow to record your responses.

Prompts

nine
Try to pinpoint emotional concerns that rob you of your thinking/planning time—negative thoughts, worries about money or family members, and any kind of pondering in–between need to be jotted down.

ten
Pull out your business calendar(s) and make a list of *every* activity, meeting and task that occupies your time. Nonsense e-mail, long lunches and listening to co-workers' troubles should be included.

eleven
Write about any of those areas where you feel out of control.

twelve
To regroup and focus on going forward, everyone needs time alone each day. Do you value time alone? How much time during the day do you take for yourself?

thirteen
Sometimes you might feel overwhelmed by your schedule, then act in negative ways because of those out-of-control feelings. List any of those behaviors. Try to pinpoint the causes of those behaviors. Are there certain triggers that bring those negative actions to the surface?

fourteen
Are you involved in any activities that do not support your deepest sense of who you are or want to be? What are they?

fifteen
What are some of the most common feelings and emotions that occupy your inner thoughts?

sixteen
Jot down any situations in which you were uncomfortable with your initial emotions and reactions to certain activities.

seventeen

Write about the times you've dismissed your feelings because you thought others would not consider them important.

eighteen

Are you experiencing any physical discomfort because of stress or exhaustion? List those symptoms and when you experience them most.

nineteen

Write about activities you're involved in that you do not care about and are doing just to please someone else.

twenty

Imagine your best friend or an adult child of yours comes to you stressed out, exhausted and seeking your advice. What would you tell that person to do to help relieve the stress and lead a simpler life?

38 | All are architects of fate, working in

these walls of time.

Henry Wadsworth Longfellow

poet

I can read! I can write! I have power!
The notion is motion. Write down your
thoughts and your spirit moves.

Nancy Robinson
newspaper columnist, pilot
and motivational speaker

All things work together for good to them that love God.

Romans 8:28

One layer at a time, one
word in a sentence, they all
peel down to the nubbin.

Pat Haley
author

When I want to understand
what is happening today or
try to decide what will happen
tomorrow, I look back.

Oliver Wendell Holmes
author

This above all else: To thine
own self be true.

William Shakespeare
playwright, poet and actor

If one advances confidently in
the directions of his dreams
and endeavors to live the life
which he has imagined, he will
meet success unimagined in
common hours.

Henry David Thoreau
author, philosopher and naturalist

Checkpoint   Many people will first feel frustrated after journaling on a few of these prompts. That's good. Feel the frustration and let it help you realize which activities and thoughts are congesting your days and mind. Those are the pebbles on the road to a simpler life—pebbles that make the path bumpier and less pleasant on a daily basis—pebbles you need to remove.

In the prologue of Mary Tyler Moore's autobiography, *After All*, Moore bares a profound inner conflict. Moore has a candid "conversation" with the television personality Mary, confessing her fears of inadequacy as well as jealousy of the beloved TV character. True to the character's accommodating nature, Mary offers reassurance, reminding Moore of her mother's favorite quote: "'We all did the best we could at the time.' So just write what comes to you."

Because of that remembered blessing, Mary Tyler Moore was able to write out her thoughts and feel the frustration of an often chaotic lifestyle. All the while she learned things about herself that she never before realized—important revelations that helped her go forward to a simpler life. You will, too.

chapter 3

Writing Through the Pain

Our whole past experience is
continually in our consciousness,
though most of it is sunk to a
great depth of dimness.

Charles Sanders Peirce

author and philosopher

In the words of the ever-popular, ever-insightful Dr. Seuss, "Unslumping yourself is not easily done." Problem is, even if you're honest with yourself about changes that need to be made in your life, listening to that inner voice is not always easy. As a matter of fact, sometimes unslumping yourself is darn excruciating.

You have to own up to certain faults. You not only have to accept responsibility, you have to be willing to stretch emotional muscles that might have atrophied over the years. It might hurt.

Pain isn't something we welcome. Yet when we're honest about our current choices involving time and family, we realize any move toward a simpler life often hinges on whether we're willing to endure that pain. There's always a certain

> No matter how hectic and upside-down our schedules, we can't let go of a pattern if we're not willing to confront why we fell into that pattern in the first place.

amount of stress or conflict involved in adjusting our lifestyles to find a healthier and happier balance. No matter how hectic and upside-down our schedules, we can't let go of a pattern if we're not willing to confront why we fell into that pattern in the first place.

Sometimes that discovery will be brought on by a growing weariness. Perhaps that nagging tired feeling finally makes you willing to confront the initial pain that comes with choosing a simpler life. Sometimes a traumatic event will trigger a painful evaluation of your current choices. The decision to confront the pain will either reaffirm that you *are* doing what really matters to you or prompt you to make new choices that will lead to a more honest lifestyle.

I was part of both situations several years ago in Oklahoma City. Walking the deserted hotel hallways at about one o'clock in the morning, I felt my stomach rumble as I entered the lounge. I had hoped I'd find peanuts or pretzels to sustain me through a late-night editing session.

Instead I found Lee. At first I pegged him for a bouncer: standing at the door guzzling a longneck, all decked out in creased black Wranglers and a starched white oxford shirt. When I asked if the lounge served any munchies, he shook his head and said, "Nope, but I'll be happy to treat you to breakfast down the road."

Something in his eyes tugged at my soul, and a few minutes later we were sitting in a nearby café, sipping coffee and learning a little about each other. He looked tired, so I asked why he'd gone to the hotel bar instead of home to sleep. It turned out that Lee, a firefighter, had just finished an exhausting two-week stretch of duty at the site of the Alfred P. Murrah Federal Building explosion.

No doubt about it, he needed sleep, yet he couldn't sleep without nightmares. He needed much more than bacon and French toast. He needed some way to filter away the pain he'd felt while rescuing mangled victims. Single and without any family to talk to, Lee had no idea how to deal with the grief from those bloody days.

Being alone wasn't what Lee feared. He even knew he'd eventually sleep again. What really worried him was the thought of going back to work. If he made himself forget the faces in his nightmares, maybe he would stop caring. If he didn't care, how could he go back to work?

Pretty heavy thoughts for someone I had considered a bouncer.

I explained to Lee that I teach people how to use writing to help heal after emotional upheavals and choose what matters. In between bites of bacon we went over a few exercises. After a while, we settled on some strategies that he believed would help him cope with the painful memories, move on into rest and later return to work.

First Lee would write descriptions of the pain—of the horrible things he saw—and then throw them away. This process would flush away the negative aspects of his job. Second, he would write his memories of saving lives or families' homes on blank business cards. These cards would counteract the gruesome tragedies he sometimes faced as a firefighter. If he felt any fear or anxiety creeping in, he'd whip those cards out of his wallet and read the positives instead.

The next day, as I thought of Lee's decision to confront his pain and affirm what he really wanted out of life, my own tired emotions flexed—then stiffened. I realized that even as an adult I'd not always risked the pain to choose what really mattered to me. Many times I'd hidden behind the same numbness I'd felt as a child whose thoughts never mattered.

Admitting that reality ripped at my psyche—so much for practicing what I preached. I wondered how on earth I could choose what really mattered to me after all those years of ignoring that kid inside me who was constantly told, "What matters to you isn't important."

That was the scary part. If I went forward, I'd have to let the kid who wasn't allowed to ask *why?* out of her emotionless shelter. And that kid would want to know why I'd taken so long to do it. I'd have to account for that.

She'd remained silent when I had chosen relationships that were unhealthy and when I had chosen to please other people—filling my days with duties that *they* thought I should assume—instead of pleasing myself. She had waited patiently every time I denied her a voice and instead gave my time to someone else.

But Lee's visit pumped up her weak inner biceps. She peeked over the tar paper walls of my soul, then knocked on the rickety door of my heart. A couple of honest jabs demolished years of emotional patch jobs I'd tried to hide with cheap plaster and second-rate priorities.

The choice was clear: I'd have to either squash her again or choose the pain that would come with the complete destruction of my inner facade. It was the only way to move forward and simplify my life.

I let her rip. And boy, did she. On notebook paper I listed every crack in the mortar of my soul. False walls crashed and crumbled, showering me with chunks of memory and accountability. No doubt about it, going backward hurt like heck.

The pain was necessary. Without walking through the rubble of that reality, there could be no rebuilding. There could be no new foundation to fortify what really mattered. And without a simplified and sturdy architecture, there could be no secure, authentic self.

Are you ready to work the soreness out of rarely used emotional muscles? If you're willing to lay a new foundation that will simplify your life, look at these prompts. Start with a few of the weighty jumping-off exercises. Before long, you'll become much stronger and more confident in choosing what is "selfishly" healthy for you.

The pain was necessary. Without walking through the rubble of that reality, there could be no rebuilding. There could be no foundation to fortify what really mattered. And without a simplified and sturdy architecture, there could be no secure, authentic self.

Prompts

Choose the prompts that interest you most, and use the blank pages that follow to record your responses.

one

Write this phrase: "I accept where I am right now and forgive myself for the choices I made in the past that have brought confusion or chaos." Describe where you are emotionally.

two

If where you are now and where you want to be differ, describe where you'd like to be emotionally.

three

Our early lives determine our self-image. List the phrases you heard most often as a child. Try to remember if any of those phrases echoed in your mind as you made adult decisions about your career, relationships or personal goals. Write about those instances.

four

Not wanting to let someone down sometimes causes us to take on or remain in relationships, responsibilities or jobs that don't feel right. List any similar situations in your life.

five

Some people believe shutting down emotionally is easier than confronting the pain of change. List any times you've chosen to ignore your feelings for the sake of keeping peace.

six

List any reasons you've chosen to live without joy or doing what you love.

seven

If any of those reasons involve a fear of the pain or conflict that may come with change, list who would be involved in the pain. List any ways those people would benefit if you chose to change your current lifestyle.

eight

Emotional stretching and goal-searching may cause a little soreness the first few times you try them. List any anxieties you're experiencing while journaling.

nine

What bothers you most about choosing to put yourself first in your life?

ten

List any phrases from your past that tell you not to choose what you have always wanted to do.

eleven

Are you allowing your time to be manipulated because you fear choosing to do what really matters to you?

twelve

As a child, were you told to think of others' needs before your own?

thirteen

If you are head of a household, do you feel you should put every wish of your family ahead of your own desires?

fourteen

Write down your perceptions of your family's needs. On that list, how many are really *needs* and how many are *wants*?

fifteen

If you're in an unhappy relationship, write down a few things that don't feel right about it. Do you feel you are responsible for the other person's happiness?

sixteen

If you had the unconditional love and support from the people you care about to follow any desire of your heart, what direction would you choose?

Prompts

seventeen

Pretend you're offering your unconditional love and support to someone facing your crossroads. What advice would you give that person?

eighteen

List any guilty or unworthy feelings you're having about wanting to do what really matters to you with your time.

nineteen

Think about how you would encourage someone you care about to deal with this type of remorse. Pretend you're writing them a letter of support, but address it to yourself and apply it to your past, present and future.

Spiritual is stronger than any 65
material force...thoughts rule
the world.

Ralph Waldo Emerson

poet

66 | For as he thinks within himself, so he is.

Proverbs 23:7

Be not afraid of life. Believe
that life is worth living and
your belief will help create
the fact.

William James

psychologist and philosopher

There is only one success—
to be able to spend your life
in your own way.

Christopher Morley
author

The longest journey is the
journey inwards of him
who has chosen his destiny,
who has started his quest.

Dag Hammarskjöld

statesman and economist

Don't let those crazies
get you. Reload with
paper and pen.

Sam Horn

literary agent and author

Whatever you can do, or think you can,

begin it. Boldness has genius, power

and magic in it.

Johann Wolfgang von Goethe
poet, novelist and playwright

✿ ✿ ✿

Checkpoint Misplaced or twisted feelings of loyalty can chain us to empty or even dangerous relationships. Sometimes they can even keep us linked to jobs we despise. Fears of the unknown anchor us in daily stress.

When these negatives multiply and mutate unchecked, physical side effects, such as heart disease or chronic headaches, often emerge. Sometimes *emotional* side effects emerge, like the numbness I felt. When you're numb, you feel nothing—no pain, but no joy, either. Until we realize we're forcing ourselves to live an unhealthy pattern—no matter how painful that realization is—we can't move forward.

And moving forward must occur if you plan on simplifying your life—even when you're not aware you're being pushed into the baby step of deciding to change. When I first met Lee as he guzzled that longneck, I had no idea he would help me see the kid who had stayed numb too long. I also had no idea the child I'd kept hidden would be so painful to release. And it was a complete surprise to discover her exhilaration as I watched her run free—charging into life with a mischievousness and air of fun she'd never been allowed. If you can brave the pain, you'll embrace the joy of a simpler life.

❀

chapter 4

Choosing a Simpler Life

You may have a fresh start at any
moment you choose, for this thing
we call "failure" is not the falling
down, but the staying down.

Mary Pickford
actress

Choosing. Again, it all comes down to choice. We either choose to
look at the realities or we choose to ignore them. We either
choose to go forward into a simpler life or we choose to stay
locked into our schedules of endless commitments while the
confusion ricochets within our weary minds.

Be prepared: your life will grow muckier before the sed-
iment of the past oozes into history. Soon after I allowed that
kid to knock her way out of numbness, the calm surface wa-
ters of my life churned into a whirlpool. My patience grew
shorter with my children, with my husband and with every
other person I dealt with through work or in the community.
Reformatting your thinking and behavior takes an incredible
amount of energy, and it wreaks havoc on your personal and
professional life.

I knew making changes wouldn't be easy. First, I had to consider my priorities. My children mattered, of course, as well as my husband. They would always be a major part of any personal decisions regarding time. But what really mattered to my growth was my writing and editing. I wanted to devote my efforts to both of these aspects of my career.

Maybe if I could spend more time concentrating on my career, I could bring more income into the household budget. Maybe if that happened, I might not have to always work a less desirable part-time job. Maybe, maybe, maybe.

This is perhaps the hardest part of choosing what matters to you. You have no guarantee of favorable outcome. You only know you're finally choosing a direction that makes you happy. Faith in the end product is a necessity, because as you go through the process of change, the picture of your future remains fuzzy.

There are only twenty-four hours in a day; I'd have to give up something to succeed in my forward motion. I might even have to give up two or three somethings. How could I do that? To be accepted at all as a kid, I had to be unselfish, to not ever think about what really mattered to me.

If I chose more time for me, well, maybe people wouldn't like me. Maybe I'd be considered rude or antisocial. Maybe choosing what really mattered would cause me to lose friends or alienate family. Again with the maybes.

The whole dilemma pounded in my head like a rushing

river slamming against granite boulders. If I didn't find a way out of the confusion, I knew my soul would suffer spiritual erosion.

I tried to tell my husband how I felt—stumbling to find the words I'd only allowed myself to write in tattered notebooks. With each confession came a rush of tears. Exhausted, I gave up on my attempt at talking and escaped to the shower.

Finally, under a spray of scalding water, I washed away the years of denial that those tears had released. Even as I did, I realized I needed to cry that hard. I needed to grieve for each time I'd wanted to bawl as a child and had been told not to. I also needed to grieve for each time, when I was an *adult*, I had not chosen what really mattered.

That reality stung worse than the boiling shower.

I was responsible for the current of chaos that threatened to tow me under. The big picture made me sad, then angry. The anger sobered me out of grief and left me eager to say, "No more."

That's step one to choosing a simpler life: Say "No more."

During the next few days I worked to keep up with my scattered thoughts. First I would make a list of what I could still do for my husband and children while working the part-time job and scraping out a few hours a day for *my* goals.

That's step two: List the necessities you're responsible for each day.

Next, I'd have to cut out being "on call" for any other people. *I* had allowed them to use me, and it was up to me not to allow it. It wasn't a question of not loving them—it was an essential need to love myself just as much, to affirm what really mattered to me.

Whatever happened because of my decision to go forward would just have to happen. There would be no going back.

That's step three: Say out loud to yourself, "I am going forward."

William James once said, "Believe that your life is worth living and your belief will help create the fact." Believing is also a choice.

Believing in your inner self and *honoring* your previously hidden priorities must go hand in hand on your journey to a simpler life.

It's amazing how fast my career fell into place after I said out loud to myself what really mattered to me. And of course, because my new career proved more profitable, I was able to give more time to my family by giving up the part-time job.

Something even more surprising happened. My family ended up respecting me, not resenting me. When my youngest sister went back to college recently, I asked what she wanted to major in. She paused for a moment and finally said, "I want to do something with graphic arts, but something on a home computer, so I can be successful with my own business like you are with yours."

Another affirmation came just before my mom died. She had been proofreading my books *Depression* and *John Grisham* before I turned them in to the publisher. Not only was it healing that *Depression* let her know I had compassion for her bipolar disorder, but the proofing she did gave me something that I had waited thirty-five years to receive.

At the time, she was healthy in spirit, but her body was wearing out. She called me a few days after sending some pages back and told me she really liked what I'd written. Less than a week later I gave the eulogy at her funeral.

Her call was the first time I'd ever heard genuine praise from one of my parents regarding anything that mattered to me. Who knows how long I would have waited if I hadn't chosen what was important to me—if I hadn't chosen to be "selfish" and go forward with what I wanted.

You must choose to go forward. It boils down to that initial baby step. Another baby step comes the first time someone asks you to run an errand for them and you say, "Sorry, can't do it, I'll be _____," filling that blank with what really matters to you.

More than anything, choosing to go forward is choosing to take action. Failure to meet commitments is not about there being too few hours in the day. Retailers feed us the latest high-tech gadgets to keep overworked, overstressed people on time and organized. But we don't need a gadget to help us meet more commitments; we need a time-out from *too many* commitments.

We need a time-out to reconnect with our inner selves and discover what matters most. If you feel your life is worth more than what an electronic gadget can categorize and itemize, then scan through these prompts. Jot down as many realities as you can so you can recognize and weed out the things that are tripping up your progress. Only then will you help yourself choose to go forward into a simpler life.

❀

one

By this point you've written down items you believed were important. Maybe they've changed during your journaling travels. Write down this phrase: "I deserve what is best for me." Now take a few moments and list what you believe the best for you means.

two

If you've never spoken out loud about what matters to you, write your reasons for making that choice in the past.

three

Write down this phrase: "I will not allow any reason to keep me from what is best for me." Visualize your idea of what is best for you. Write down those thoughts.

four

Make a list of the time-consuming activities you'll sacrifice for what matters to you.

five

List the new things you'll do to attain what matters most.

six

"The negative aspects of choosing this direction will not keep me from achieving my goal because..."

seven

"The positive aspects of choosing what is best for my life will help my family and friends because..."

eight

"The worst thing that could happen if I choose to go forward is..."

nine

"The worst thing that can happen to me if I choose *not* to go forward is..."

Prompts

Choose the prompts that interest you most, and use the blank pages that follow to record your responses.

Prompts

ten
"I might disappoint some people, such as…"

eleven
"To choose a different direction means major change, such as…"

twelve
Write down this statement: "Even if the changes first bring chaos, I believe that the eventual joy and satisfaction will be worth the turmoil." Write down the things you think will be worth the chaos. What will you have to confront—and move through—on the path toward choosing what matters to you?

thirteen
The reasons you'd encourage someone else to go forward are…

fourteen
How would you encourage someone else to react to disapproving comments?

fifteen
List the reasons you would encourage someone to confront possible turmoil and disapproval from friends in order to change a lifestyle and choose what's best for that person.

sixteen
Write and say out loud, "I deserve to go forward. I choose to go forward." Write at least two of your own affirmations to remind yourself that you deserve a simpler life and that you will choose a simpler life.

seventeen
Write and say out loud, "My first step is…"

eighteen
Those who know us best also know what buttons to push to manipulate us. List any triggers you recognize that could detour you on your journey.

nineteen

Visualize ways to take control of your move forward. One way may be simply to spend at least three lunch hours each week on your own. Another might be to screen your phone calls during your family time. Make a list of new boundaries—protective lines you'll draw—that will keep people from stealing your time or burdening you with guilt.

twenty

Study your new boundaries. If you think you'll experience any guilt over your decisions, write about those potential feelings.

twenty-one

Write down what you'd say to your friends on the rough days after their commitment to change...on the days they falter and consider giving up what matters to them.

92 |

God respects me when I
work, but He loves me
when I sing.

Rabindranath Tagore

poet, painter, mystic and musician

I am not bound to win, but I am bound to be true...to live up to what light I have.

Abraham Lincoln
former president of the U.S.

Our concern must be to live
while we're alive—to release
our inner selves from the
spiritual death that comes
with living behind a facade
designed to conform to
external definitions of who
and what we are.

Elisabeth Kubler-Ross

psychiatrist and author

Your pain is the breaking | 99
of the shell that encloses
your understanding.

Khalil Gibran

essayist and philosopher-poet

100 | Dream lofty dreams, and as you dream, so shall you become. Your vision is the promise of what you shall at last unveil.

John Ruskin

art critic, author and reformer

Shoot for the moon. Even if you miss it, you will land among the stars.

Les Brown

motivational speaker and author

Hold fast to dreams for if dreams die, life is a broken-winged bird that cannot fly.

Langston Hughes

author and poet

Checkpoint   I will admit my path wasn't easy. There were stumbles and a few bruises from some rough falls. Some friends wouldn't tolerate my decision to spend more time on me. I'm happier without them.

My journey took me to a peak from which I could look back and see how choosing "selfishly" made joy accessible. Sometimes, when I tried to jog ahead too fast, I ran out of steam. Those were the times I told myself it was OK to rest beside the quieter river and dabble my toes in the cool water.

You'll have days such as those. You'll have days that are just the opposite, when you'll climb a tall pine and breathe in such freshness that you'll believe you can fly. Those are days that make the journey to a simpler life worth that initial difficult choice.

Choices. It's all about choices.

❀

chapter 5

Enjoying the Simpler Life

What I do today is important because
I am exchanging a day of my life for it.

Hugh Mulligan
author

Never forget you are in charge of each new day. *Each* new day. You
can choose a chaotic life or a simple life. But you can't choose
a simple life without first tuning in to your spirit. Without a
simplified inner self, you will never have a simplified outer life.

I certainly do not equate simplicity with being devoid of
complex thoughts and passions. Those are necessary for a
healthy inner self. Simple means cutting to your basic
desires—not just once in your life, but with every sunrise.

Nourishing your inner spirit each morning is as important as that first glass of energy-laden orange juice. It's a necessary habit for optimum emotional health, just as regular
exercise is a necessary habit for optimum physical health.

Let's say you've made the big commitment. You've reeval-
uated where you are in life. You've probed your emotions with
the prompts in this book. You've made the commitment to
move forward. You're feeling better. You're less stressed. You're

discovering you really do remember how to grin. Good for you.

Then your boss asks you to take on another project. Your neighbor needs help with a garage sale. Your child's Little League team needs another volunteer to make phone calls.

Perhaps a tragedy trips you up. Someone in your family faces a crisis, and you become the listener and adviser or the gofer and the caretaker. Bit by bit, your schedule begins creeping out of control again. How do you stay grounded in what really matters? How do you hold on to your simplified life?

Remember to rely on those boundaries you drew up for yourself in the last journaling section. If you don't choose what really matters to you, then you're constantly reacting to other people's desires. You're denying yourself access to your soul.

Two people come immediately to mind. They had never met before, and they were from completely different backgrounds. Karen was well-educated, a wife and young mother who said she'd come to class strictly as moral support for a friend who had also enrolled. A man named John, recently divorced, said he had come because he was a songwriter. He didn't need any of that "mumbo-jumbo, whiner stuff," but he hoped to use the writing tips for his songs.

Karen's newborn baby had recently died and she was working through her grief even as her husband and family members denied that she should be grieving at all. This was her life chaos. Her support system kept telling her that what mattered to her wasn't important. One night she opened up to

the class and told us she felt suffocated, that she never cried
and that she believed she had to pretend that there never had
been a child to grieve.

John rarely spoke during class, and when he did he always cracked a joke or talked about his songs. His songs, however, echoed love—the kind of love that dangled just out of his
reach. He couldn't say out loud to us how he felt about his lost
marriage, but he never hesitated to sing us a song that layered
his feelings in rhythm and music.

The last night of class—a class which neither had ever
admitted they needed—John sang a song he'd written for
Karen and her numbness.

Softly, reverently, his lyrics whispered of loss and busy-
ness and the need to look within. They spoke of really appreci-
ating the people you love and not dismissing their worth. Each
phrase encouraged people to see behind vacant eyes—to view
how lonely it would be to smile a lie when what they needed
was the right to choose what really mattered.

That night Karen cried. And John no longer denied.

Later they both sent me letters telling me how much the
writing class had helped them go forward. Two separate lives,
two similar needs.

Their family and friends had told them to just keep them-
selves busy, to just get on with life, to just let go of their troubles. Letting go is impossible until you connect with why you
are drowning in either emotional pain or chaotic confusion.

Many people have learned to avoid emotional confusion by pumping up their inner selves every day. Gwen Choate, a much published author and editor of *Women Forged in Fire*, has learned that choosing what really matters to her is easier if she simplifies her concerns each morning. She says,

> In the front of my journaling notebook, I have three small plastic bags. Inside each bag are small square pieces of paper. Squares in Bag #1 list names of people and situations I have concerns about and for which I say prayers. Squares in Bag #2 are my "Thank you" blessings where I offer thanks over things that have been resolved. Squares in Bag #3 are my "Nit" items. Little stuff goes on them, like someone who has an irritating habit that pushes my buttons and I want to stop reacting. You'd be surprised how fast those get cleared out!

Each day, she prays over the past and new squares, eliminating any that have been resolved. By confronting these concerns daily, she's able to move forward.

Hiding will not work to clear confusion, and sometimes you do have to give a little extra time to others. But often you can learn to say yes to your feelings and no to those tugs on your time. Granted, it will take practice. That's what your journaling is for.

one

Write a list of affirmations that center on the positive aspects of your inner self. Begin with these phrases: "I will pledge daily to choose what is best for myself" and "Choosing what matters to me helps me love myself, and that helps me love others."

two

Make a list of all the ways you're generous with your time, even when you don't say yes to every request for it.

three

Once again, write out the goals you've chosen and follow each with the phrase: "I will accomplish this goal by..."

four

Write out this phrase: "It is not selfish for me to want my goal. It is necessary." Give reasons why you believe your goals are necessary.

five

Begin three sentences with "My goal will benefit me because..."

six

Make a list of three people with whom you'll share your goal. Jot down three different reasons for choosing those people.

seven

What are the main reasons you won't share your goal with certain people? Write those down.

eight

Study the reasons behind any negative comments you believe you may hear from certain people. Write down adjustments you might need to make to your boundaries, keeping this new insight in mind.

Prompts

Choose the prompts that interest you most, and use the blank pages that follow to record your responses.

Prompts

nine

Take a few minutes and close your eyes. Visualize what you need to do today to make your goals into realities—jot down any new ideas.

ten

Make a list of all the positive things people have said or you have read that have to do with your choosing what matters to you.

eleven

Write down this commitment: "I will prescribe for myself a daily routine of writing out the positives and negatives of the things that matter the most to me." Now jot down your list for today.

twelve

Consider stashing "victory items," such as cards from friends or favorite photos of family members, in your journal. These will help you see glimpses of joy amidst some of the emotional gunk. Make a quick list of items that come to mind.

thirteen

Imagine you've finally chosen what matters to you, but have run into negative reactions from someone. Write what would you say to that person—but never, never, never send angry letters!

fourteen

Sometimes this exercise will spur memories of past situations that made you angry—write about those, too, and purge the anger you may have repressed. Again, *never* send angry letters. Scribble through them afterward or tear them up, but never send them.

fifteen

Write about how you felt after confronting your anger and doing something to acknowledge it.

sixteen

Fast-forward five years: name some things that will be different about your lifestyle if you continue to choose what really matters to you.

seventeen

Write down your reasons for choosing this book.

eighteen

Write down the unexpected things you've discovered about yourself through the process of journaling.

nineteen

If there are still issues to ponder, write them down...and then take yourself back through the process of confronting and writing through an issue to discover what really matters to you.

Far away in the sunshine
are my highest inspirations.
I may not reach them,
but I can look up and see
the beauty, believe in them,
and try to follow where
they lead.

Louisa May Alcott
author

The truth shall make you free.

John 8:32

Writing about historical people makes me realize we each have a deeper story to tell. Our lives are important to someone–especially to us.

Ann Arnold

author, historian and lecturer

Now I'm beginning to live a little, and feel less like a sick oyster at low tide.

Louisa May Alcott

author

From his cradle to his grave
a man never does a single
thing which has any first
and foremost object save
one–to secure peace of
mind, spiritual comfort for
himself.

Mark Twain
author and humorist

Leisure and the cultivation of human capacities are inextricably interdependent.

Margaret Mead
cultural anthropologist and author

It is easier to live through
someone else than to
become complete yourself.

Betty Friedan

feminist and author

When I saw my thoughts
on paper, I met a person I
hadn't known.

Frank Ball
author

Checkpoint In Tim Allen's book *I'm Not Really Here* he writes, "This book is a culmination of a five-year journey of self-discovery." He didn't realize when he started the autobiography that he would learn so much about himself.

I've read dozens of similar passages in other autobiographies. Each one proves that people have learned the impact of journal writing. The popular actress Helen Hunt says she uses journal writing as therapy, writing out things about all aspects of life that require a lot of thought and attention.

When you write in a journal, you can't help but simplify your life, because you'll be writing from an honest perspective. You'll become more aware on a regular basis of what really matters to you.

Life *should* be enjoyed in a simple way, even when it's full of complex insight and rich textures. As you take up your pen, I wish for you a path of fresh blessings while you journal toward a simpler life. And if you wander through any of my forests, be sure to stop and share a little of what really matters to you—but don't take too long. After all, I'll be rambling on to the next piney shadow, exploring what new things might really matter to me.

❀